FANTASTIC STRUCTURES

A COLORING BOOK OF AMAZING
BUILDINGS REAL AND IMAGINED

STEVE McDONALD

CHRONICLE BOOKS

SAN FRANCISCO

This book is dedicated to everyone who loves to color.

Although many of the images have been drawn from my own photographic sources, I want to also acknowledge and thank the following photographers for the wonderful images used in part for some of the drawings: **Jeremy Blakeslee** (Kennecott Mines); **Flavio Bruno** (Chrysler Building Detail); **Frédéric Chaubin** (Celebration Palace of Rituals); **Kai Friis** (Kuggen); **Craig Hiemburger** (Concrete Dream); **Michael Hill, aka Doctor Comics** (Fuji Television Building); **Dennis Jarvis** (Alexander Nevsky Cathedral, Pelişor Castle, Saint Basil's Cathedral); **Rick Ligthelm** (Jubilee Church, Montevideo Residential Building , Neuer Zollhof); **Tosh Marshall** (Battersea Power Station); **Jeffery Milstein** (LAX Terminal from Above); **David Monniaux** (Old Town Edinburgh Homes); **Heribert Pohl** (Neuschwanstein Castle, Zollern Colliery); **Rob Shephard** ("The Gherkin" and City Buildings).

ISBN: 978-1-4521-5323-0
Manufactured in China

Illustrations by Steve McDonald
Designed by Neil Egan

10 9 8 7 6 5 4 3

Chronicle Books LLC
680 Second Street
San Francisco, CA 94107
www.chroniclebooks.com

Chronicle books and gifts are available at special quantity discounts to corporations, professional associations, literacy programs, and other organizations. For details and discount information, please contact our premiums department at **corporatesales@chroniclebooks.com** or at 1-800-759-0190.

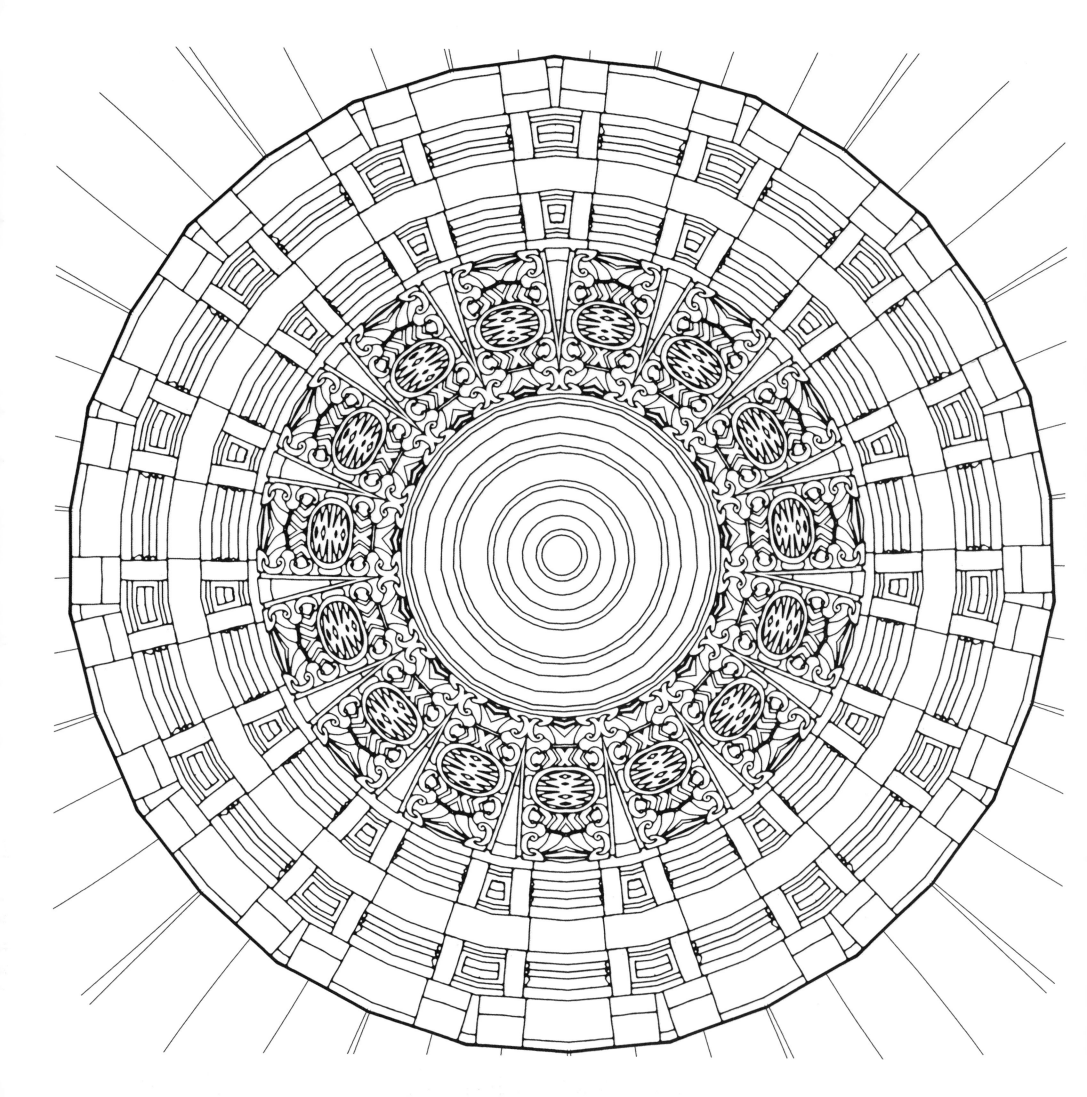

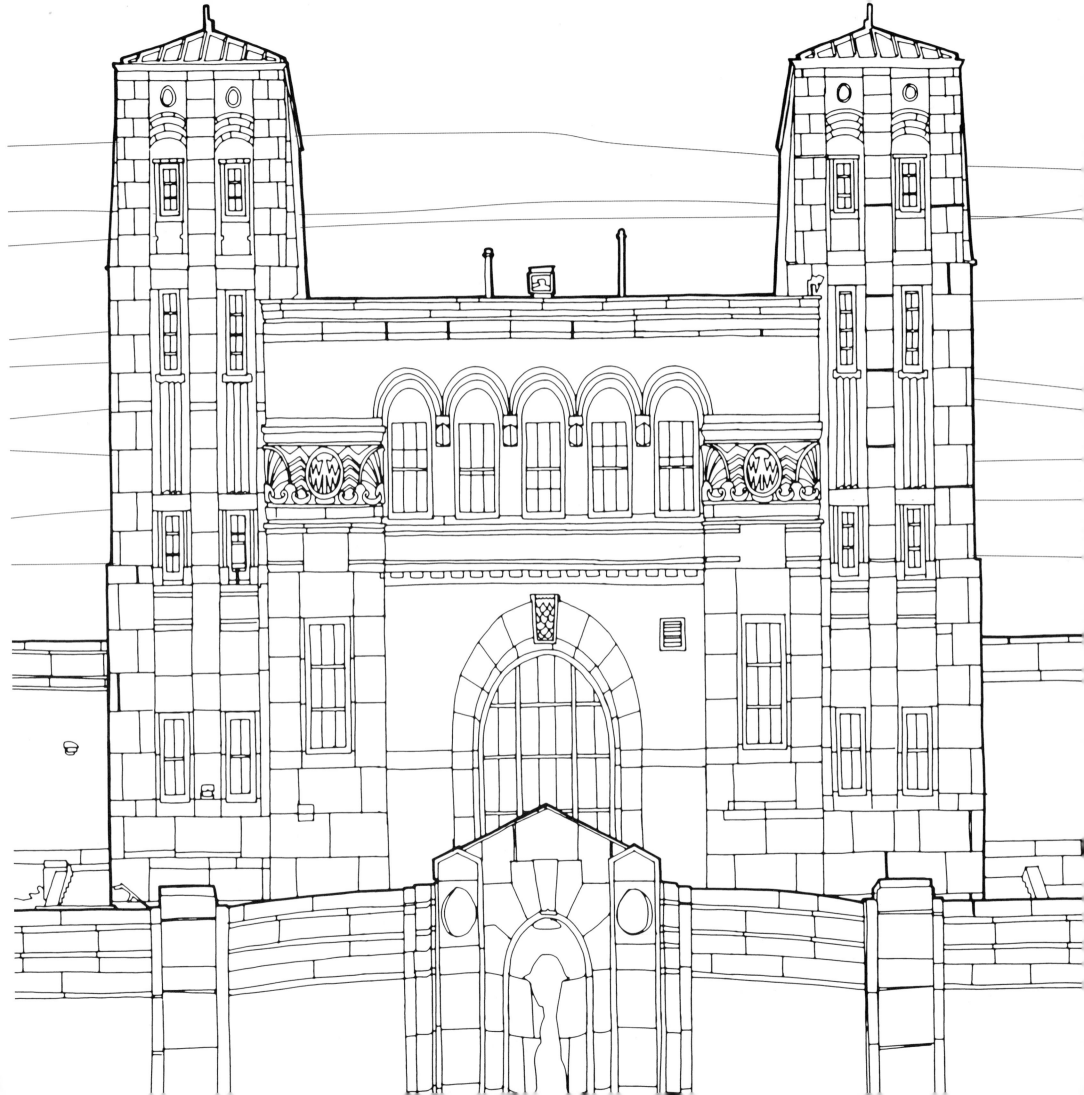

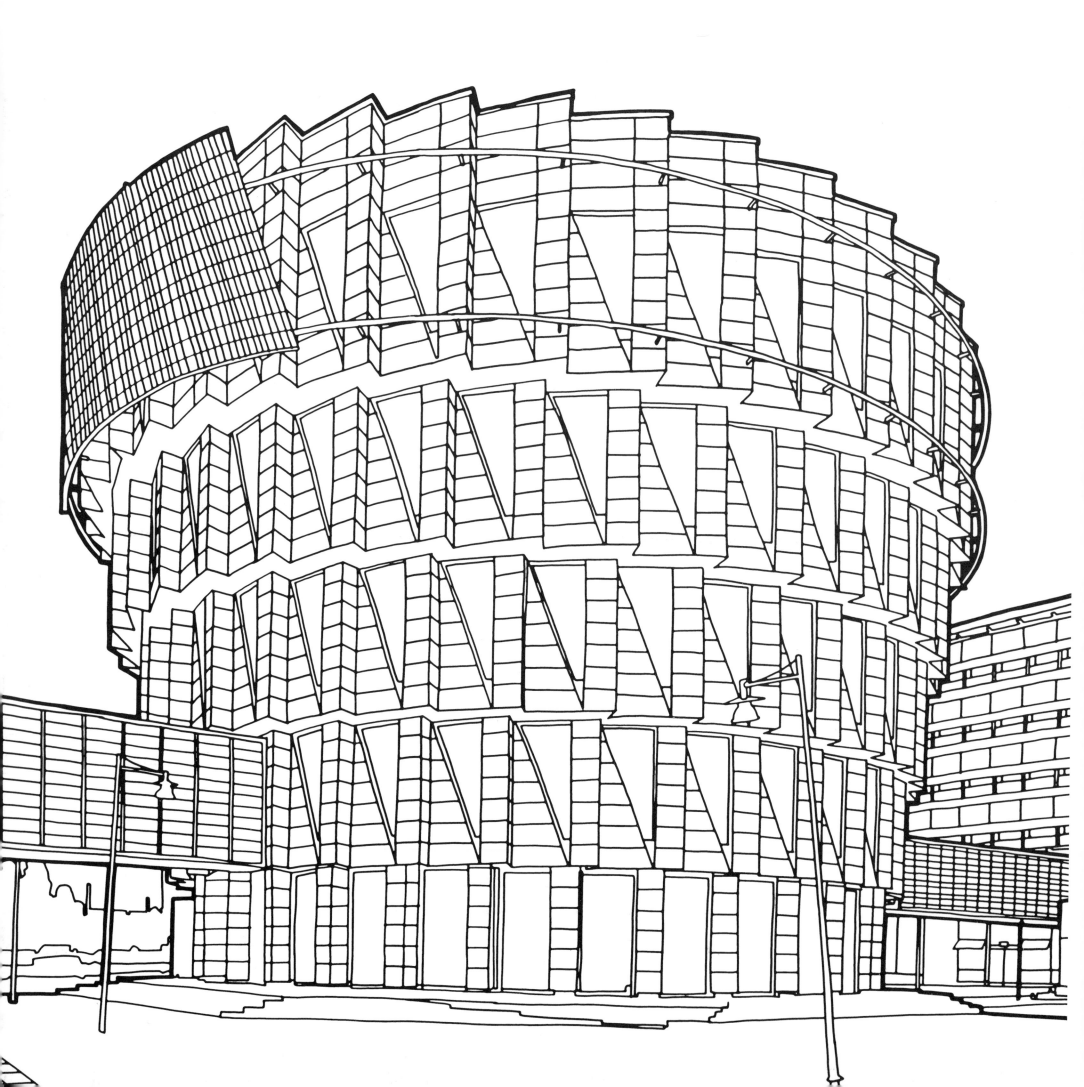

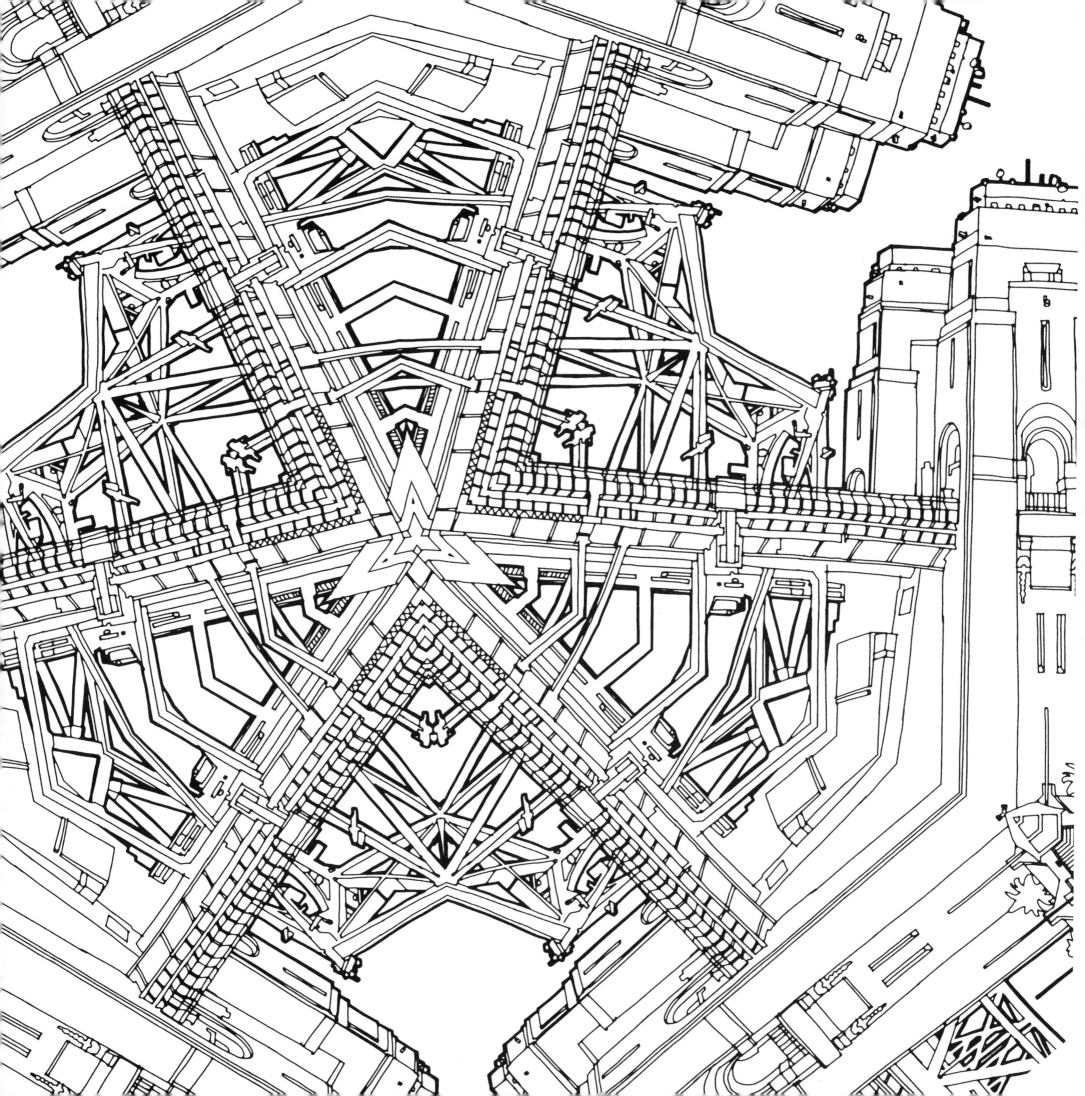

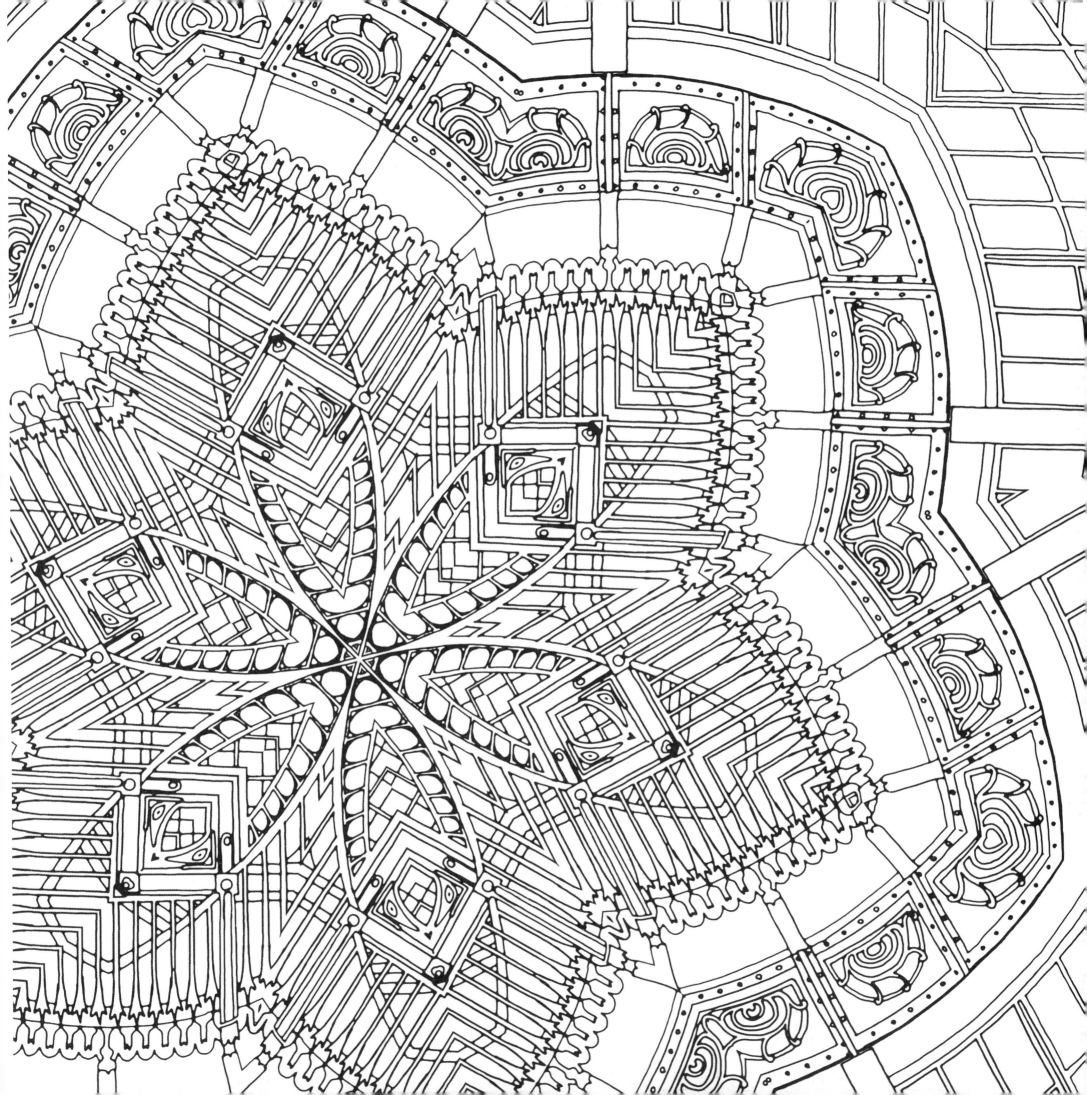

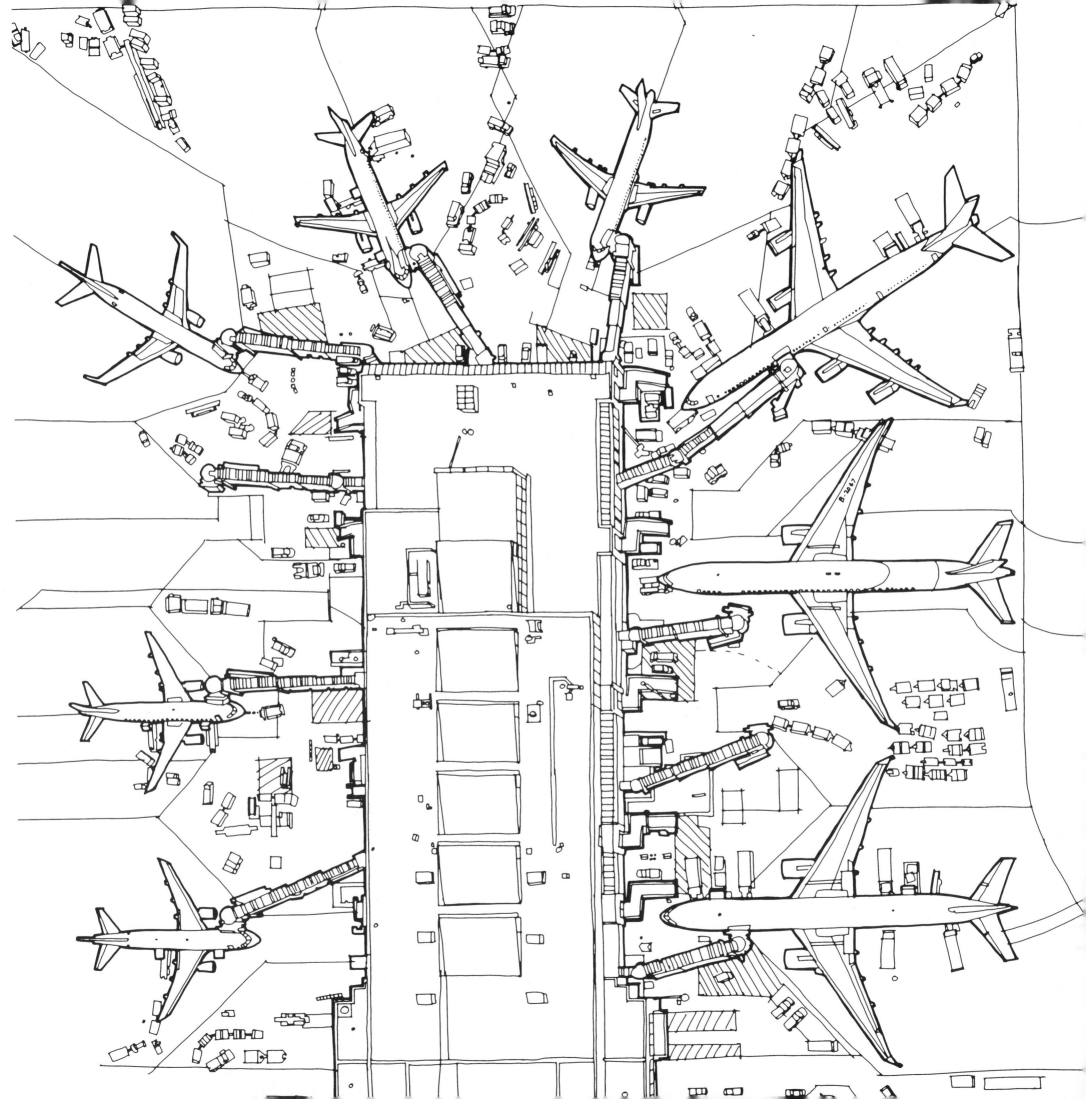

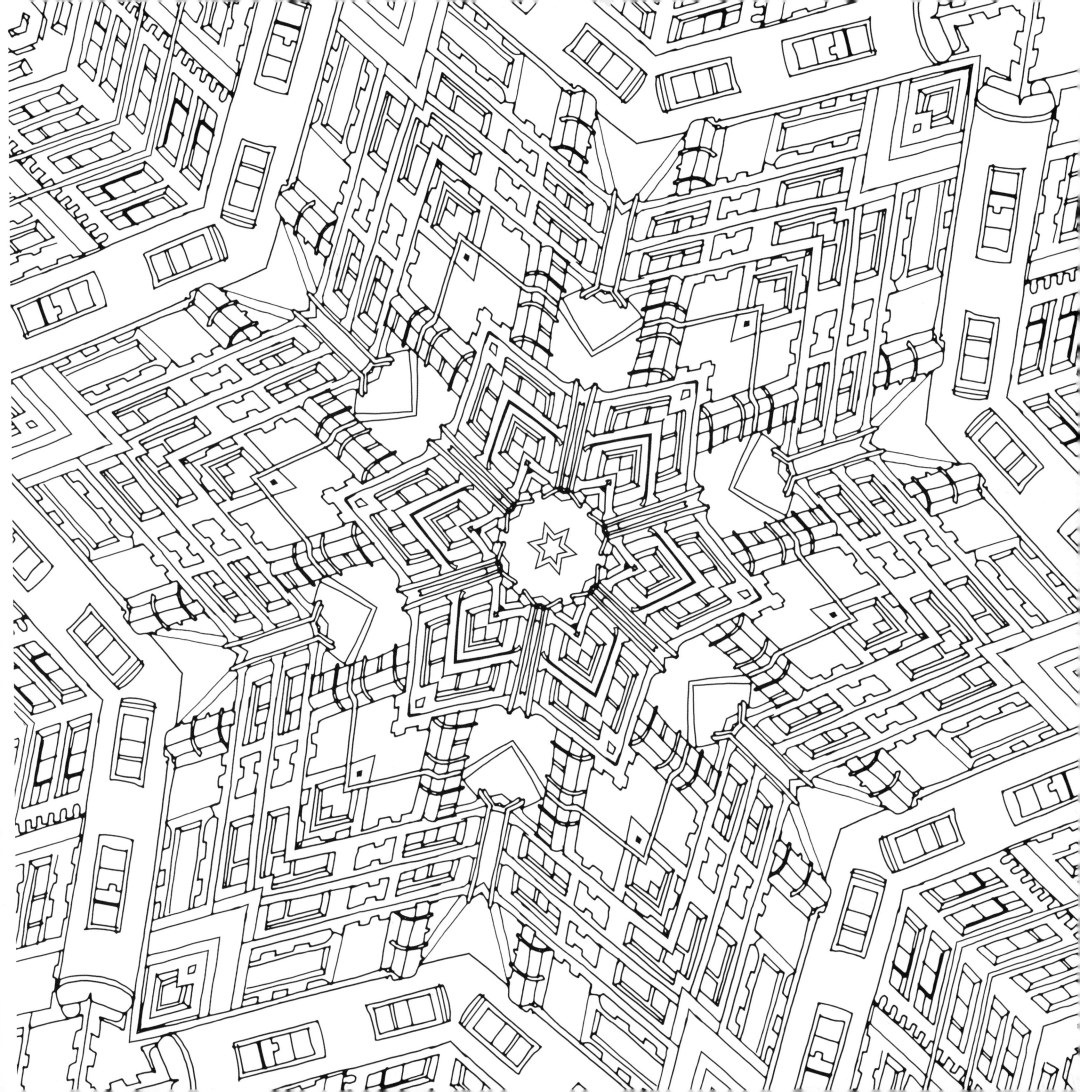

Latin Cathedral and Cathedral Square, Lviv, Ukraine ◀